STO

COMETS

SAMANTHA BONAR

COMETS

A FIRST BOOK
FRANKLIN WATTS
A Division of Grolier Publishing
NEW YORK / LONDON /HONG KONG / SYDNEY
DANBURY, CONNECTICUT

Photographs ©: AP/World Photos: 42, 44 top; Art Resource: 53 left (Bridgeman), 53 right (Giraudon) 8 (Erich Lessing), 25; Astronomical Society of the Pacific: 13 (Dennis Mammana), 19; Corbis-Bettmann: 24; Jon Lomberg: 22; NASA: 18; Photo Researchers: 29 (Julian Baum), 16, 46 bottom (Chris Butler), 39 (Clark Et Al./Mcdonald Observatory/SPL), 51 (European Space Agency/SPL), 38 (David A. Hardy), 10, 34 (Mehau Kulyk), 48 top (Dennis Milon), 46 top (Pekka Parviainen), 48 bottom (John Sanford), 41 (Jerry Schad), 26 bottom (Frank Zullo); Stock Montage, Inc.: 9 (Charles Walker Collection); Stocktrek Photo Agency: 15 (Frank Rossotto), 20; Stocktrek Photo Agency/Finley Holiday Film: 27; Stocktrek Photo Agency/Mt. Wilson: 30; Stocktrek Photo Agency/NOAO/ Lowell Observatory: 55; Stocktrek Photo Agency/Soviet Academy of Science: 32

Visit Franklin Watts on the Internet at:
http://publishing.grolier.com

Library of Congress Cataloging-in-Publication Data

Bonar, Samantha.
    Comets / by Samantha Bonar.
        p. cm.—(A First Book)
    Includes bibliographical references and index.
    Summary: Describes what has been learned about the composition, orbits, and the existence of several well-known comets.
ISBN 0-531-20301-8 (lib.bdg.)   0-531-15907-8 (pbk.)
    1. Comets—Juvenile literature.   [1. Comets.]   I. Title.   II. Series.
QB721.5B66 1998
523.6—dc21   96-53502   CIP
                                                                            AC

CONTENTS

"EVIL STARS"

CHAPTER 1

On October 14, 1066, two powerful rulers met on a battlefield in southern England. One of them, King Harold, had seized the English throne. The other, Duke William of Normandy, thought he was the rightful king of England. He had sailed from France to fight for the crown.

The battle between the two rulers' armies was swift and bloody. Harold was killed, and William became king of England. King William's descendants ruled the land for the next 400 years.

Before the battle, many English people had predicted that Harold would lose. It was not because Harold's army was tired from fighting Norwegian invaders just before battling

Comets were once thought to be signs of
disasters to come. In this 1,000-year-old
tapestry, King Harold's men point with fear to
an approaching comet. Soon after, the king
was killed in the Battle of Hastings,
and the comet was blamed.

William. It was not because William's army was better equipped. Though these things were true, the English thought Harold faced defeat because of something they had seen in the sky.

"DISASTERS"

A few months before the battle, a brilliant *comet* as large as the full moon had appeared in the night sky for a month. In those days, peo-

A 400-year-old drawing showing a comet terrifying the people of a German city

Today we know that a comet cannot predict or cause future events—it is simply a huge ball of frozen water, gases, and dust that orbits the sun.

ple did not appreciate a comet's beauty. They thought a comet was a sign of a disaster soon to come: a plague, drought, flood, famine, earthquake—or the death of a king.

The word "disaster" comes from two Greek words: *dis*, meaning "evil," and *astrum*, meaning "star." People thought comets were disasters, or evil stars. The 1066 comet, which we now know was an appearance of Comet Halley, seemed enormous to viewers on Earth. According to one account, it was "an omen of doom, such as no man had ever seen before." King Harold's defeat, however, had nothing to do with the comet.

Today we know that comets are not disasters. These striking visitors from the farthest reaches of our *solar system* have no effect on Earth's affairs. Comets do not predict or cause future events—but they might be able to tell us about Earth's distant past. Many astronomers believe that comets hold secrets to how our solar system was formed and how life on Earth began.

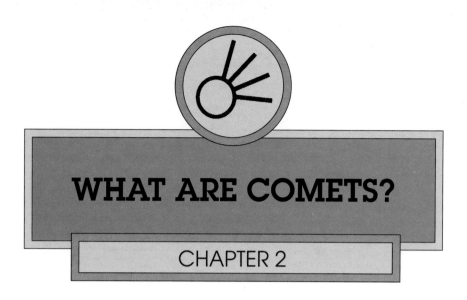

WHAT ARE COMETS?

CHAPTER 2

Ever since the first recorded comet sighting in China more than 4,000 years ago, people have been fascinated and terrified by these balls of light that set the night sky ablaze. Because they seemed to come out of nowhere and appeared irregularly, comets made people nervous. No one knew what to make of these strange visitors in the familiar sky.

ANCIENT BELIEFS

A comet often looks like a fuzzy ball in the sky. It may appear to be bigger than the moon. Sometimes a comet looks like a ball with a long *tail* streaming from it like hair. The word "comet"

Some comets are bright enough to
be visible to the naked eye.

comes from the Greek word *kometes*, which means "long-haired." People in ancient times believed that comets were "long-haired" stars.

Aristotle, a Greek philosopher who lived about 2,000 years ago, thought that comets were pieces of burning air that caused drought and strong winds. People believed this theory for centuries, until a sixteenth-century Danish astronomer named Tycho Brahe used math to prove that comets were farther away from Earth than the moon. He showed that comets are not part of our atmosphere—they are millions of miles away.

"DIRTY SNOWBALLS"

Today, most scientists believe that comets are as old as our solar system, which was formed about 4.6 billion years ago. They think that comets are chunks of material left over from the formation of the planets in our outer solar system—Uranus, Neptune, and Pluto.

It is very cold in the outer solar system. The surface temperature of Pluto, the planet farthest from the burning sun, is about −382°F (−230°C). Most comets can be found in an area far beyond Pluto. We see a comet only when some-

A comet may look like a fuzzy ball,
sometimes with a tail.

thing—such as the gravitational pull of a passing star—sends it toward the center of our solar
system. Because of the way comets look and
act, scientists believe they are huge balls
of frozen water, gases, and dust. In 1950, an

An illustration of what a comet
might look like up close

astronomer named Fred Whipple described
comets as "dirty snowballs."

Because comets are among the oldest bodies
in our solar system, they may carry important
clues about how our solar system formed. Some
scientists believe that crashing comets brought
water and gases to Earth billions of years ago,
helping to form our atmosphere and oceans. It

is also possible that comets carried some of the organic materials necessary for life to begin on Earth. Without comets, we might not exist.

ANATOMY OF A COMET

The front of a comet, which consists of the *coma* and the *nucleus*, is called the head. It is made of gases (mostly ammonia, methane, and water) and dust. The head may be hundreds of thousands of miles wide.

The nucleus is the solid part of the comet. It may be one piece, or several pieces held together by gravity. It may measure from a fraction of a mile wide to 10 miles (16 km) wide. The nucleus of a comet has been seen only once, when the spacecraft *Giotto* flew right through the head of Comet Halley and photographed its nucleus in 1986. *Giotto's* photos showed that Halley's nucleus was a lumpy ball of ice about 9 miles (14.4 km) long and 5 miles (8 km) wide.

The coma is the part of the head that has *sublimed*, or transformed directly from a solid to a gas without passing into a liquid state. A comet's coma can be larger than the sun, which is 864,000 miles (1,390,176 km) wide.

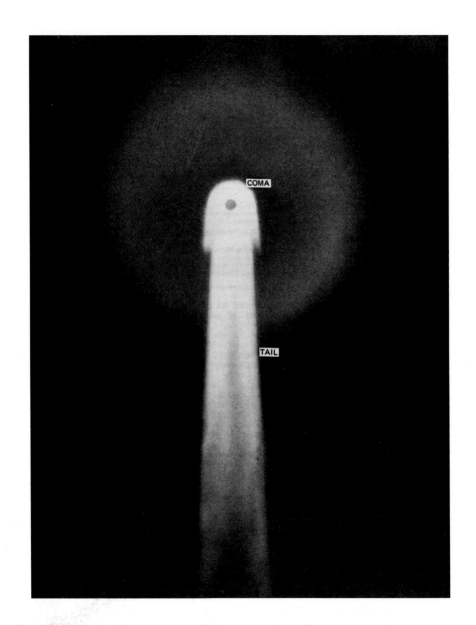

A diagram of the parts of a comet

The nucleus of Comet Halley was
photographed by the spacecraft *Giotto* in 1986.

The tail is a trail of gas and dust attached to
the head. It can stretch as long as 100 million
miles (160.9 million km) and can take different
forms. If a tail is straight and blue (a "Type I"
tail), it is made mostly of gas. If it is curved and
yellow (a "Type II" tail), it is made mostly of dust.

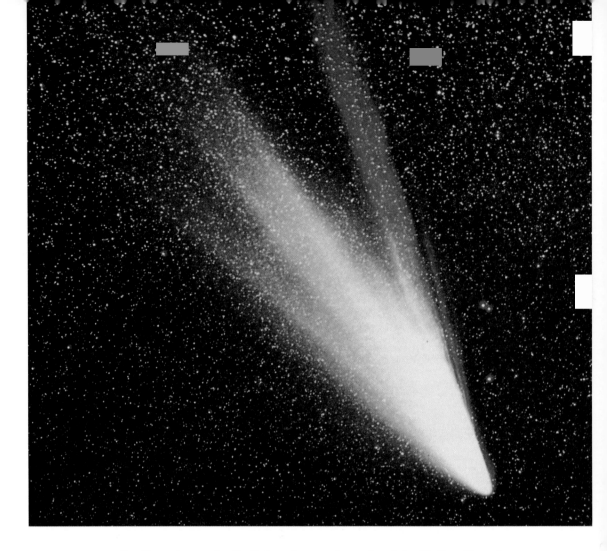

Both a gas tail (blue) and a dust tail (yellow)
are visible in this photograph of Comet West.

A comet can also have more than one tail. A
comet with "no less than six or seven tails,"
according to a contemporary account, was
seen in 1744.

THE OORT CLOUD

CHAPTER THREE

Comets seem to appear and disappear in the sky like mysterious ghosts. Their appearances are not random, however. Comets are travelers on very definite paths.

MILLIONS OF COMETS

Astronomers aren't sure exactly where comets come from. But a Dutch astronomer named Jan Oort suggested in 1950 that there is a vast, misty cloud at the outermost edges of our solar system. The cloud is made up of gases, dust, and comets floating in space like icebergs float in the sea. Scientists estimate that the *Oort cloud* is 3 trillion miles (5.5 trillion km) away from the sun and contains millions of comets.

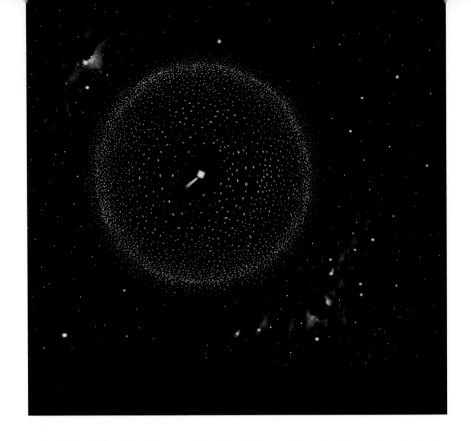

In this illustration of what the Oort cloud might look like, the bright spot in the center represents our solar system as far as the orbit of Pluto.

THE KUIPER BELT

The *Kuiper Belt* is a wide area of comets just beyond the planet Neptune. A comet was first discovered in this region in 1992. In 1994, the Hubble Space Telescope picked up faint images of comets here. The Hubble data suggests that the Kuiper Belt may be home to millions of comets.

The Kuiper Belt is changing some of our beliefs about the outer solar system. Pluto and its moon Charon may be part of the Kuiper Belt. Some of the frozen moons belonging to the outer planets may also have come from the Kuiper Belt.

There is some new evidence that a smaller, narrow belt of comets may lie between Uranus and Neptune. This belt is a possible storehouse of *short-period* comets—comets that *orbit* the sun at least once every 200 years.

There is also new evidence that our solar system might not be the only one that is home to comets. Some scientists believe that the disk of gas and dust that surrounds the star Beta Pictoris may contain comets, too. Evidence suggests that a few hundred comets a year plunge toward this young, nearby star.

JOURNEY TOWARD THE SUN

Every year, the gravitational force of passing stars forces 200 or so comets in toward the center of the solar system. Most of these comets are too small to be seen from Earth with the naked eye.

An illustration showing the path (pink arrow)
around the sun taken by Comet Kohoutek

The comets have their orbits changed as they
move closer to the sun. The closer a comet gets
to the sun, the faster it moves. Because of the
sun's gravitational pull, the comet cannot move
past the sun. Instead, it must go *around* the sun.
Passing around the sun makes the comet go
even faster. It is now going fast enough to head
away from the sun and back toward outer
space.

English astronomer Edmond Halley discovered that comets travel in elliptical orbits around the sun. He theorized that comets that had appeared in 1456, 1531, 1607, and 1682 were actually reappearances of the same comet. He also predicted that this comet would return in 1758. It did—and was named Halley in his honor.

Some comets travel only once around the sun before they are destroyed. A few comets actually hit the sun and are destroyed instantly.

Other comets are "grabbed" by the gravity of one of our solar system's nine planets. When this happens, the comet will travel back and forth between the sun and that planet's orbit until so much ice evaporates that the comet falls apart.

Seventeenth-century scientists Edmond Halley and Isaac Newton discovered that a comet will go around the sun, then out to the planet's orbit, and then back toward the sun in a long and narrow, or elliptical, orbit. Caught between the sun's and the planet's gravity, it will trace this hot-dog-shaped path again and again. Some comets make this trip only once or twice. Others may travel back and forth more than 100 times.

SHORT-PERIOD AND LONG-PERIOD COMETS

Jupiter, the largest and most massive planet in our solar system, has the strongest gravitational pull, so many comets orbit around the sun and Jupiter. Although most comets are in orbits that last several hundred years, comets that have been "captured" by Jupiter circle the sun every few years. These comets—of which we have seen about 100—are known as members of Jupiter's "family."

Comets that return to circle the sun every 200 years or less are called "short-period" or "periodic" comets. "*Long-period*" comets travel much farther and may take thousands of years to return to the sun. Right now, scientists know of about 100 short-period comets and 600 long-period comets. Comet Halley, which reappears every 76 years, is the most famous short-period

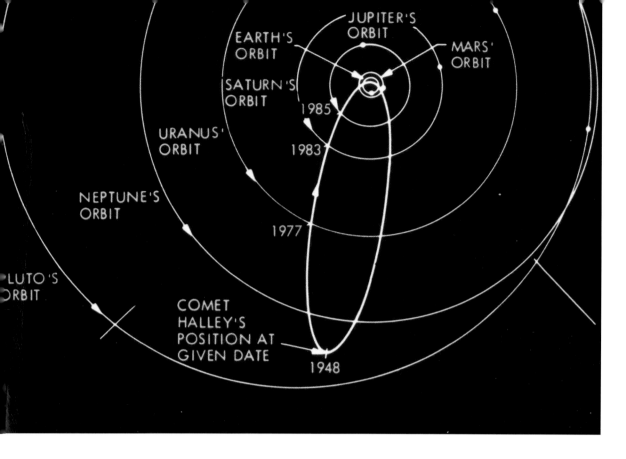

EARTH'S ORBIT

JUPITER'S ORBIT

MARS' ORBIT

SATURN'S ORBIT

1985

URANUS' ORBIT

1983

NEPTUNE'S ORBIT

1977

PLUTO'S ORBIT

COMET HALLEY'S POSITION AT GIVEN DATE

1948

A diagram of the orbit of Comet Halley

comet. It is a member of the planet Neptune's "family."

The point in a comet's orbit when the comet is nearest to the sun is called its "*perihelion*." When a comet is farthest from the sun, it is at its "*aphelion*" point. A comet usually is brightest when it is at its perihelion, but generally can't be seen because it is in the glare of the sun. A comet usually appears brightest to us just before or just after it is closest to the sun.

FORMATION OF THE TAIL

In the outer solar system, the typical comet is only a nucleus—a solid chunk of ice about 5 to 10 miles (8 to 16 km) wide. When a comet starts its journey far away from the sun, it is a dark object. Think of ice cubes. If you stand in a dark closet with an ice cube in your hand, it is invisible. But if you take the ice cube outside and hold it up to the sun, it will shine brightly.

As the comet gets closer to the sun, we are able to see it—not only because it is nearer, but because it reflects light from the sun. As the comet nears the sun it heats up. The frozen water and gases sublime into gas, forming the fuzzy coma. As the comet gets closer and closer to the sun, *solar wind* (charged particles sent away from the sun at high speeds) blows on the coma, stretching it into the comet's tail.

When the comet is approaching the sun, the solar wind pushes the tail so that it streams behind the coma and nucleus. But when the comet is moving away from the sun, the solar wind pushes the tail in front of the coma and nucleus, so the comet travels tail-first.

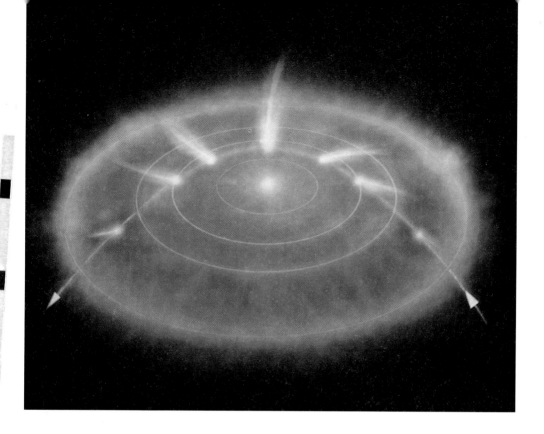

This drawing shows one comet in different positions of its orbit. The length and direction of the tail changes as the comet travels around the sun and is shaped by solar wind.

Every time a comet passes the sun, more of its material is burned off, shrinking the comet. Short-period comets are generally dimmer than long-period ones, because they pass the sun more frequently and so lose more material. The burned-off gases and dust float in the solar sys-

April 26　April 27　April 30　May 2　May 3　May 4　May 6

Halley's Comet in 1910

This is how Comet Halley looked on different days during its 1910 appearance.

tem for a very long time. Like old soldiers, comets don't really die—they just slowly fade away.

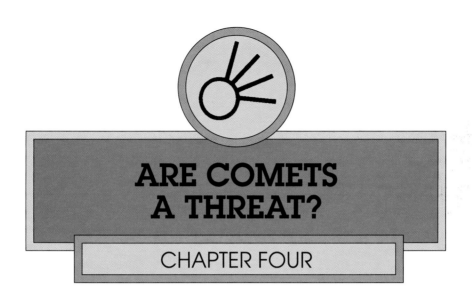

ARE COMETS A THREAT?

CHAPTER FOUR

On June 30, 1908, a tremendous explosion rocked the Tunguska region of Siberia in central Russia. The explosion was so powerful that instruments in England—3,400 miles (5,471 km) away—were affected. The jolt uprooted and flattened trees for hundreds of miles in all directions and killed entire herds of reindeer.

What caused the explosion? There was no evidence of a bomb, earthquake, or volcanic activity.

THE TUNGUSKA EVENT

It took scientists nearly 50 years to offer an explanation about what had caused the

Many scientists believe that the massive
damage in the Tunguska region of Siberia in
1908 was the result of a comet exploding high
in the air above the region.

destruction in Siberia, known as the "Tunguska Event." In 1960, Russian scientists announced their belief that a comet several miles wide and weighing about 1 million tons was the source of the explosion. The comet didn't hit Earth; it blew up high in the air. But the force of that mid-air explosion—equal to about 1,000 nuclear bombs, or 10 to 20 megatons of TNT—caused massive damage.

Evidence found in 1996 supports the Russian scientists' conclusion. A team of Italian scientists discovered tiny particles from either a comet or *asteroid* embedded in trees where the Tunguska Event occurred.

DID A COMET KILL THE DINOSAURS?

Has a comet ever actually *hit* Earth? Many scientists believe that a comet or asteroid about 3 miles (4.8 km) wide crashed on Earth 65 million years ago. Like comets, asteroids formed as our solar system was being created. Most of these huge rocks can be found in an asteroid belt between Mars and Jupiter.

Scientists believe they have located the crater caused by this comet or asteroid crash on Mexico's Yucatan Peninsula. They think that the impact threw a huge cloud of dust into the air

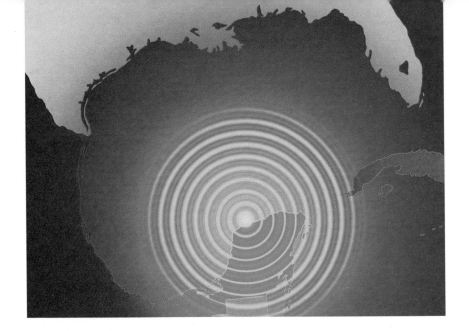

Scientists believe they have located the crater caused by a comet or asteroid crash 65 million years ago in the Yucatan Peninsula.

that blocked out the sun's light for months, maybe years, producing what is called a "global winter."

Because they need sunlight to survive, many plants on Earth died, as did the dinosaurs who lived on plants. Then the dinosaurs who ate plant-eating dinosaurs died, too. All in all, about 70 percent of the species then living on Earth disappeared very quickly.

Large comets and asteroids can cause such terrible destruction because of their incredible speed. They move at thousands of miles an hour. When such a fast-moving object hits something, it explodes with tremendous force.

NEAR-EARTH OBJECTS

Today, scientists estimate that an *NEO* (Near-Earth Object, meaning a comet or asteroid) may hit Earth about every 300,000 years. The amount of destruction an NEO causes depends upon its size, speed and landing place. Most NEOs fall in the ocean and kill no one. An NEO has never in recorded history hit a populated area. In the last several hundred years, the closest a comet has come to Earth is 1.4 million miles (2.25 million km) away. That was Comet Lexell, in 1770.

Still, scientists are concerned about NEOs hitting Earth. In 1991, the House Committee on Science and Technology of the United States Congress House of Representatives decided to address this danger. "The chances of the Earth being struck by a large [NEO] are extremely small," the Committee wrote, "but since the consequences of such a collision are extremely large, the Committee believes it is only prudent to assess the nature of the threat and prepare to deal with it."

In 1994, the Committee directed the National Aeronautics and Space Administration (NASA) and the Department of Defense to identify and catalog all comets and asteroids that are greater than 0.6 mile (1 km) in diameter and are in an orbit around the sun that crosses the orbit of Earth. Scientists estimate that an NEO would have to be this large to cause worldwide damage. As many as 1,700 NEOs of this size may cross Earth's path.

As a result, NASA and the United States Air Force launched the Near-Earth Asteroid Tracking (NEAT) program. NEAT's goal is to conduct a complete search of the sky for near-Earth comets and asteroids.

A computer-controlled telescope with an electronic camera searches for the potentially deadly space objects. It sits 2 miles (3.2 km) above the clouds on top of Mount Haleakala on the island of Maui in Hawaii. In December 1995, the telescope began scanning the sky for 12 nights each month. In just 1 year, the telescope detected 5,898 NEOs, including 3,170 never seen before.

According to White House science adviser Dr. John Gibbons, the NEAT program should have a full map of all major NEOs within 20 years. After the map is created, if scientists find a NEO heading for Earth, they estimate that we will have years, maybe decades, to figure out how to deal with it. According to Congress' 1991 statement, "We have the technology. . . to prevent their [NEOs] collision with the Earth." That might involve using nuclear weapons or rockets to destroy an NEO in space or to change its path.

COMET SHOEMAKER-LEVY

The biggest fireworks display in July 1994 was deep in outer space. Around July 21, over a 6-day period, 21 comet fragments known as Comet Shoemaker-Levy smashed into the planet Jupiter with the force of 100 million megatons of TNT—that's 10,000 times the power of all the nuclear weapons on Earth. It has been called the most violent event in our solar system in recorded history.

Although some of the fragments were as large as 2.5 miles (4 km) across, they were "like flies hitting a car's windshield," said astronomer Paul Chodas. Jupiter wasn't damaged because it is the biggest planet in our solar system—more than 1,000 times bigger than Earth.

Unlike Earth, Jupiter has no solid parts—it is a

An illustration of fragments of Comet Shoemaker-Levy entering the atmosphere of Jupiter in 1994

ball of gas and liquid. When the comet fragments entered Jupiter's atmosphere, they exploded into giant fireballs, some as large as Earth. Using telescopes, astronomers could see these tremendous fireballs. Although Jupiter wasn't damaged, it made scientists realize just how powerful a comet collision could be.

According to Dr. Chodas, it is very unlikely that a comet as large as 2.5 miles (4 km) across will hit Earth. He adds that none of the comets astronomers know of are on a collision course with Earth. He says, however, "It's the ones we don't know of that we worry about—the ones that are out there that we haven't spotted yet. Still, it's not something we should lose sleep over."

This infrared image of Jupiter shows four impact sites (yellow patches at bottom) of fragments of Comet Shoemaker-Levy.

DUSTY TRAILS

There are three or four comets in our sky every night, but they are too faint to be seen with ordinary eyesight. A comet that can be seen with the naked eye appears only about once in a decade.

Many comets that are missed by our eyes can be easily seen with binoculars or telescopes, however. In fact, many comets are discovered not by professional astronomers, but by ordinary people. That's because a professional astronomer's work usually involves studying just one particular area of the sky. Amateur astronomers more often use their telescopes to scan the entire night sky, looking for a variety of interesting things.

Comet Hale-Bopp could be spotted easily during the spring of 1997.

**Comet discoverers
Thomas Bopp (left)
and Alan Hale (right)**

HOW COMETS ARE NAMED

Comets are named after the people who find them—and that could be you! When someone thinks that they have spotted a comet, they send a telegram or an e-mail message to the International Astronomical Union (IAU) in Cambridge, Massachusetts. Within hours, the IAU will verify the finding and decide on a name.

Sometimes a comet is discovered at the same time by different people. When this happens, the comet is named after the first two or three finders—like Comet Whipple-Bernasconi-Kulin in 1942 or 1996's Comet Hale-Bopp.

There is an exception. When a stupendous comet appears, it is named "Great," like the Great Comet of 1843. Only three or four "great" comets occur in a century. The most recent one was the Great Comet of 1976.

AMATEUR COMET HUNTERS

Regular people find comets all the time. Hale-Bopp, one of the brightest comets of the twentieth century, was discovered in 1996 by two amateur astronomers.

Alan Hale, one of the finders, is a serious amateur astronomer. He has spent more than 400 hours looking for comets. But Tom Bopp, the other discoverer, is a very casual comet hunter. He doesn't even own a telescope. He discovered the comet while looking through a friend's telescope.

Comet Hyakutake, another impressive comet, was discovered in 1995 by an amateur Japanese astronomer named Yuji Hyakutake. He spotted the comet through binoculars.

FINDING COMETS

The best time to look for comets is between the hours of midnight and 6:00 A.M. There should be

Amateur astronomer Yuji Hyakutake (above) discovered an impressive comet (below) in 1995.

little or no moonlight and no clouds in the sky. The night sky is especially clear after a rain-storm, so that is a good time for comet-tracking. Choose an open space, away from trees, build-ings, and streetlights. A park is a good place. Spend about 20 minutes letting your eyes adjust to the darkness.

Most comets look like stars—they shine brightly and you can't see them moving. So how will you know if you've spotted one? You will have to observe the suspected comet over several nights. If its position changes from night to night, then it is most likely a comet. A change in position means that it is actually moving. A star always stays in one spot.

METEOROIDS

You can also keep an eye out for *meteoroids*, some of which are pieces of comets. (Other meteoroids are pieces of asteroids.) As comets melt, they leave behind some rocks and metals. If these rocks and metals collide with Earth's atmosphere, they are called meteoroids. Most meteoroids are no bigger than a grain of sand.

When a meteoroid hits Earth's atmosphere, we see a streak of light race across the night

A meteor against a starry sky at dusk

An illustration of a meteorite hitting the ground

sky. We commonly call these *meteors* "shooting stars" or "falling stars." As many as 200 million meteoroids bright enough to be seen enter our sky every 24 hours.

They usually completely burn up about 60 miles (96.5 km) above the ground. If a piece of a meteoroid makes it to the ground, it is called a *meteorite*. Only about 10 percent of meteoroids make it to Earth's surface.

METEOR SHOWERS

Sometimes, a whole bunch of meteoroids enter Earth's atmosphere at the same time. When this happens, we see a a *meteor shower*. After about 100 orbits, comets melt completely, and all that is left is a trail of dust and pebbles in space. Earth passes through about 24 trails of "dead" comets on its yearly journey around the sun. Then the sand and pebbles enter our atmosphere and produce a meteor shower.

Most meteor showers occur at the same time every year. They are named for the star constellations from which the meteors seem to come. This point of origin is called the meteors' *radiant*. For example, a meteor shower that hits every December comes from an area of sky near the constellation Gemini. This group of

A false-color photograph of a
Leonid meteor shower

This long-exposure photograph captures a
Geminid meteor (long, bright streak). The short
diagonal streaks are star trails.

meteors is called the Geminids. Sometimes, you can see more than 50 Geminids per hour.

The Leonids, near the constellation Leo, shower down in November. The source of the Leonid meteors is a comet called Tempel-Tuttle. A Leonid shower in 1966 produced more than 100,000 meteors per hour over the central United States.

The best time of year to see a meteor shower is during the first 2 weeks of August, when the Perseids (near the constellation Perseus) fall. If you look up into a dark, clear sky during this period, you are likely to see several meteors per hour.

About 4,000 pounds (1,814 kg) of dust from meteor showers fall to Earth every night. That's not just ordinary dirt under your feet—it's cosmic dust that has traveled from the farthest ends of our solar system!

THE CHAMPOLLION PROJECT

CHAPTER SIX

Scientists can learn a lot about comets from observing them from the ground. Using telescopes, cameras, calculators, and computers, they can figure out how big comets are, how fast they are moving, where they have come from, and where they are going.

Scientists learned even more from sending five spacecraft to meet Halley's Comet in 1986. Pictures and data transmitted by the spacecraft verified that a comet's nucleus is a frozen ball of water, gases, and dust. The Hubble Space Telescope's pictures of Comet Hyakutake in 1995 verified more about comets, such as the presence of water vapor in their tails.

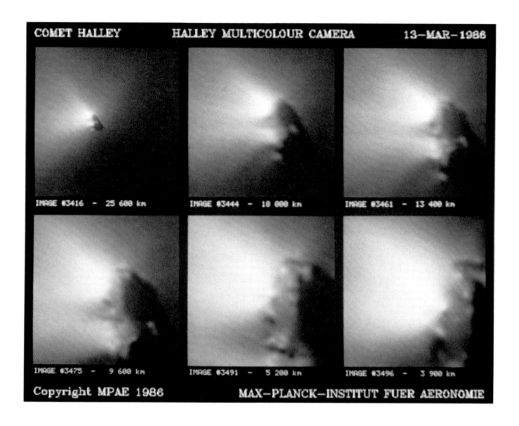

COMET HALLEY   HALLEY MULTICOLOUR CAMERA   13-MAR-1986

IMAGE #3416 - 25 600 km   IMAGE #3444 - 18 000 km   IMAGE #3461 - 13 400 km

IMAGE #3475 - 9 600 km   IMAGE #3491 - 5 200 km   IMAGE #3496 - 3 900 km

Copyright MPAE 1986   MAX-PLANCK-INSTITUT FUER AERONOMIE

By sending spacecraft to meet and photograph
Comet Halley in 1986, scientists were able to
verify that a comet's nucleus is indeed a frozen
ball of water, gases, and dust.

We have observed comets from the ground
for centuries. We have sent spacecraft into the
sky for an up-close look. What's next?

LANDING A SPACECRAFT ON A COMET

That may sound like science fiction, but such a mission is in the works. It is called the Champollion Project.

Champollion is the name of the 100-pound (45-kg) rover that will land on the nucleus of Comet Wirtanen, which was discovered in 1948. The rover will be carried into space by a spacecraft called *Rosetta*.

Why the names "Champollion" and "Rosetta"? Archaeologists discovered ancient Egyptian writings (hieroglyphics) on stones centuries ago, but had no idea how to read this strange language. In 1799, a stone was found in the Egyptian city of Rosetta. Written on the Rosetta Stone was the key to understanding hieroglyphics. In a similar way, astronomers hope the *Rosetta* spacecraft will provide the key to understanding comets.

The person who figured out how to read the Rosetta Stone was a Frenchman named Jean-François Champollion (1790–1832). Like the man Champollion, the *Champollion* lander will do the work of analyzing mysterious data.

Rosetta will be launched on January 22, 2003. It will follow Wirtanen on its trip toward

THE ROSETTA STONE

Just as Jean-François Champollion "cracked the code" of the Rosetta Stone, scientists hope that the spacecraft named after him will unlock some of the mysteries of comets.

the sun and is expected to catch up with the comet by August 25, 2011. *Rosetta* will release *Champollion* just a few kilometers above the comet's surface. *Champollion* will land on Wirtanen within 3 hours.

When *Champollion* reaches the nucleus's surface, it will immediately begin its 84-hour mission of collecting data. The lander will be equipped with a drill to dig up samples of the comet. It will analyze these samples and send data to *Rosetta* about the comet's temperature, what its nucleus is made of, and other factors. *Rosetta* will transmit this data to scientists on Earth. After 84 hours, *Champollion*'s batteries will run out and the mission will be over.

WHAT SCIENTISTS HOPE TO LEARN

Getting an actual sample of a comet will tell scientists exactly what comets are made of. By studying this sample, they may unlock the secrets of the formation of the solar system and the origins of life itself.

Comets have changed very little since our solar system formed 4.6 billion years ago. Comets are like 4.6-billion-year-old time capsules. They are made of the ancient gas and dust from which the planets were formed.

A computerized color image of Comet Halley
taken in 1910. This famous short-period comet
will make its next appearance in the year 2062.

If scientists can figure out the exact nature of these gases and dust, they may be able to unlock the secret of how our planets were created.

Comets also may hold the answer to the origins of life in our solar system. Scientists believe that crashing comets carried water to planets. They also think that comets may carry carbon-based molecules, which are the basis of life.

Some new evidence supports this theory. NASA now has photographs proving that every day, about 40,000 "house-sized" snowballs from outer space hurtle earthward. As they strike Earth's upper atmosphere, they transform into large clouds of water vapor. As one scientist notes, this "relatively gentle cosmic rain and its possible simple organic compounds may well have nurtured the development of life on our planet."

Those dirty snowballs that ancient humans called disasters, or evil stars, may instead be our "lucky stars." Perhaps one day we will know enough about comets to be able to thank our "lucky stars" for the gift of life.

THE COMET HALL OF FAME

Shortest period—Encke's Comet; it returns to our part of the solar system every 3.3 years.

Longest period—Comet Delavan; in 1914, the comet came close to the sun and then sped back to the outer solar system, not to return for 24 million years.

Longest visit—A comet in 1811 was visible in the sky for 18 months.

Longest tail—The tail of the Great Comet of 1843 stretched 200 million miles (321 million km).

Greatest number of tails—A comet in 1744 was said to have at least six or seven tails.

Bigger than the moon—In 1770, a comet appeared as a fuzzily shining ball four times as big as the moon.

Bigger than the sun—The head of the Great Comet of 1811 was larger than the sun.

GLOSSARY

Aphelion—The point in a comet's orbit when the comet is farthest from the sun

Asteroid—Rocky objects, most of which orbit between Mars and Jupiter

Coma—The cloud of gas, dust, and water vapor that surrounds a comet's nucleus

Comet—A frozen ball of water, gases, and dust from the farthest reaches of our solar system

Ellipse—The long, narrow shape of a comet or planet's orbit

Kuiper Belt—An area of comets just beyond the planet Neptune

Long-period—Term used to describe a comet that has a period longer than 200 years

Meteor—The light that you see in the sky when a meteoroid enters Earth's atmosphere

Meteorite—A meteoroid that lands on Earth

Meteoroid—A particle of dust or rock that enters Earth's atmosphere

Meteor shower—A group of meteors

NEO—An acronym that stands for Near-Earth Object. An NEO can be a comet or an asteroid

Nucleus—The solid, frozen part of a comet

Oort cloud—A vast cloud that lies at the outermost

edges of the solar system and contains gases, dust, and comets

Orbit—The curved path of a comet or planet as it moves around the sun

Perihelion—The point in a comet's orbit when the comet is closest to the sun

Period—The time it takes a comet to complete one orbit

Radiant—The area of the sky from which a meteor shower originates

Short-period—Term used to describe a comet whose period is 200 years or less

Solar system—The solar system is made up of the sun, nine planets (Mercury, Venus, Earth, Mars, Jupiter, Saturn, Uranus, Neptune, and Pluto), moons, asteroids, comets, gases and dust

Solar wind—Particles, made up mostly of hydrogen gas, that are sent away from the sun at high speeds in all directions

Sublime—To transform directly from a solid to a gas, without passing through a liquid state

Tail—The long part of a comet; it is made of gases, dust, and water vapor

TO FIND OUT MORE

BOOKS AND ARTICLES

Berger, Melvin. *Star Gazing, Comet Tracking, and Sky Mapping*. New York: G.P. Putnam's Sons, 1985.

Broad, William J., "As Space Rocks Whiz by Earth, Search for Dangers Gets Serious,"*New York Times,* May 14, 1996.

"Comet May Be Brightest to Pass so Close to Earth Since 1556," *Los Angeles Times,* March 7, 1996.

Couper, Heather. *Comets and Meteors*. New York: Franklin Watts, 1985.

"Light Fantastic: Comet Hyakutake Expected to Be Brightest in 20 Years,"*Los Angeles Times*, March 21, 1996.

Moore, Patrick.*Comets and Shooting Stars*. Brookfield, CT: Copper Beech Books, 1995.

"New Comet Moves Like a Comet but Looks Like an Asteroid," NASA press release, August 22, 1996.

"Responding to the Potential Threat of a Near-Earth-Object Impact," AIAA Position Paper (1995).

Stone, Richard, "The Last Great Impact on Earth," *Discover*, September 1996.

ONLINE SITES

Due to the changeable nature of the Internet, sites appear and disappear very quickly. These resources offered useful information on comets at the time of publication.

Comet Hale-Bopp Home Page

http://www.jpl.nasa.gov/comet/
Information, links, and thousands of images of the most spectacular comet of the 1990s.

Comet Observation Home Page

http://encke.jpl.nasa.gov/
Great source of information on comets in general, as well as specific comets. Photos, links, and glimpses into space for the next comets heading our way.

Comets

http://www.windows.umich.edu/comets/comets.html
Learn all about comets on a beginner, intermediate, or advanced level. Text has embedded links for more details. Images, charts, books, and lots of "cool stuff."

Comets and Meteor Showers

http://medinfo.wustl.edu/%7Ekronkg/index.html
Provides accurate positions of each current visible comet, online star charts, and information on historical comets.

Educators' Guide to Kitchen Comets

http://bang.lanl.gov/solarsys/edu/comets.htm
A complete recipe for creating your very own comet nucleus. It's messy, so tell your teacher or parent about it first!

INDEX

Numbers printed in *italics* indicate llustrations.

ABOUT THE AUTHOR

Samantha Bonar is an editor at *The Los Angeles Times* and a freelance writer. Her articles for children have appeared in *American Girl*, *Boys' Life*, *Highlights*, *National Geographic World*, *Ranger Rick*, *3-2-1 Contact*, and many other publications.